Broad Grins by George Colman the Younger

COMPRISING, WITH NEW ADDITIONAL TALES IN VERSE, THOSE FORMERLY PUBLISH'D UNDER THE TITLE
"MY NIGHT-GOWN AND SLIPPERS."

"DEME SUPERCILIO NUBEM."

George Colman the Younger was born on 21st October 1762, the son of George Colman the Elder, a noted and successful playwright and translator of Terence and Plautus among others.

Colman was educated at Westminster School before going on to University at Christ Church, Oxford, and then King's College, University of Aberdeen, before finally proceeding to Lincoln's Inn, London to become a student in Law.

In 1782 his first play 'The Female Dramatist' was premiered at his father's Haymarket theatre.

It appears that as early as 1784, Colman had entered into a runaway marriage with an actress, Clara Morris, to whose brother David Morris, he eventually sold his inherited share in the Haymarket theatre.

After her death he wrote many of the leading parts in his plays for Mrs Gibbs (née Logan), whom he was said to have secretly married after the death of his first wife.

His father, George Colman the Elder, was by now in failing health and was obliged to relinquish to his son the management of the Haymarket theatre in 1789, at a yearly salary of £600. Although Colman sought to emulate and build on the success of his father he was not quite of the same caliber.

On the death of his father in 1794, the Haymarket patent was continued to the son; but difficulties arose in his path, he was involved in litigation with Thomas Harris, and was unable to pay the running expenses of the performances at the Haymarket. In dire circumstances Colman was forced to seek sanctuary within the Rules of the King's Bench Prison. Although he would continue to manage the affairs of the theatre he would reside here for several years.

Released at last through the kindness of George IV, who had appointed him exon. of the Yeomen of the Guard, a dignity that Colman soon liquidated to the highest bidder.

In 1824 he was made examiner of plays by the Duke of Montrose, then the Lord Chamberlain. This granting of office caused widespread controversy amongst his peers who were appalled at his severe censorship and illiberal views, especially as his own works were often condemned as indecent. Apparently at times even the words 'heaven' and 'angel' were deemed to be offensive by him.

George Colman the Younger held this office until his death in Brompton, London on 17th October 1836 at the age of 73. He was buried alongside his father in Kensington Church.

Index of Contents

ADVERTISEMENT

My Booksellers inform'd me, lately, that several inquiries had been made for My Night-Gown and Slippers,—but that every copy had been sold;—they had been out of print these two years.—"Then publish them again," said I, boldly,—(I print at my own risk)—and with an air of triumph. Messrs. Cadell and Davies advise'd me to make additions.—"The Work is, really, too short," said Messrs. Cadell and Davies,—"I wish, gentlemen," return'd I, "my readers were of your opinion."—"I protest, Sir," said they, (and they asserted it, both together, with great emphasis,) "you have but Three Tales."—I told them, carelessly, it was enough for the greatest Bashaw, among modern poets, and wish'd them a good morning. When a man, as Sterne observes, "can extricate himself with an equivoque, in such an unequal match,"—(and two booksellers to one poet are tremendous odds)—"he is not ill off;"—but reflecting a little, as I went home, I began to think my pun was a vile one,—and did not assist me, one jot, in my argument;—and, now I have put it upon paper, it appears viler still;—it is execrable.—So, without much further reasoning, I sat down to rhyming;—rhyming, as the reader will see, in open defiance of all reason,—except the reasons of Messrs. Cadell and Davies.—

 Thus you have My Night-Gown and Slippers, with Additions, converted to Broad Grins;—and 'tis well if they may not end in Wide Yawns at last! Should this be the case, gentle Reviewers, do not, ungratefully, attempt to break my sleep, (you will find it labour lost) because I have contributed to your's.

GEORGE COLMAN, the Younger.
May, 1820.

MY NIGHT-GOWN AND SLIPPERS

Tom, Dick, and Will, were little known to Fame;—
No matter;—
But to the Ale-house, oftentimes, they came,
To chatter.

It was the custom of these three
To sit up late;

And, o'er the embers of the Ale-house fire,
When steadier customers retire,
The choice Triumviri, d'ye see,
Held a debate.

Held a debate?—On politicks, no doubt.
Not so;—they care'd not who was in,
No, not a pin;—
Nor who was out.

All their discourse on modern Poets ran;
For in the Muses was their sole delight;—
They talk'd of such, and such, and such a man;
Of those who could, and those who could not write.

It cost them very little pains
To count the modern Poets, who had brains.
'Twas a small difficulty;—'twasn't any;
They were so few:

But to cast up the scores of men
Who wield a stump they call a pen,
Lord! they had much to do,—
They were so many!

Buoy'd on a sea of fancy, Genius rises,
And like the rare Leviathan surprises;
But the small fry of scribblers!—tiny souls!
They wriggle thro' the mud in shoals.

It would have raise'd a smile to see the faces
They made, and the ridiculous grimaces,
At many an author, as they overhaul'd him.
They gave no quarter to a calf,
Blown up with puff, and paragraph;
But, if they found him bad, they maul'd him.

On modern Dramatists they fell,
Pounce, vi et armis—tooth and nail—pell mell.
They call'd them Carpenters, and Smugglers;
Filching their incidents from ancient hoards,
And knocking them together, like deal boards:
And Jugglers;
Who all the town's attention fix,
By making—Plays?—No, Sir, by making tricks.

The Versifiers—Heaven defend us!
They play'd the very devil with their rhymes.

They hope'd Apollo a new set would send us;
And then, invidiously enough,
Place'd modish verse, which they call'd stuff,
Against the writing of the elder times.

To say the truth, a modern versifier
Clap'd cheek by jowl
With Pope, with Dryden, and with Prior,
Would look most scurvily, upon my soul!

For Novels, should their critick hints succeed,
The Misses might fare better when they took 'em;
But it would fare extremely ill, indeed,
With gentle Messieurs Lane and Hookham.

"A Novel, now," says Will, "is nothing more
Than an old castle,—and a creaking door,—
A distant hovel;—
Clanking of chains—a gallery—a light,—
Old armour—and a phantom all in white,—
And there's a Novel!

"Scourge me such catch-penny inditers
Out of the land," quoth Will—rousing in passion—
"And fy upon the readers of such writers,
Who bring them into fashion!"

Will rose in declamation. "'Tis the bane,"
Says he, "of youth;—'tis the perdition:
It fills a giddy female brain
With vice, romance, lust, terror, pain,—
With superstition.

"Were I Pastor in a boarding-school,
I'd quash such books in toto;—if I couldn't,
Let me but catch one Miss that broke my rule,
I'd flog her soundly; damme if I wouldn't."

William, 'tis plain, was getting in a rage;
But, Thomas dryly said,—for he was cool—
"I think no gentleman would mend the age
By flogging Ladies at a Boarding-school."

Dick knock'd the ashes from his pipe,
And said, "Friend Will,
You give the Novels a fair wipe;
But still,
While you, my friend, with passion run 'em down,

They're in the hands of all the town.

"The reason's plain," proceeded Dick,
"And simply thus—
Taste, over-glutted, grows deprave'd, and sick,
And needs a stimulus.

 "Time was,—(when honest Fielding writ)—
Tales full of Nature, Character, and Wit,
Were reckon'd most delicious boil'd and roast:
But stomachs are so cloy'd with novel-feeding,
Folks get a vitiated taste in reading,
And want that strong provocative, a Ghost.

"Or, to come nearer,
And put the case a little clearer:—
Mind, just like bodies, suffer enervation,
By too much use;
And sink into a state of relaxation,
With long abuse.

"Now, a Romance, with reading Debauchees,
Rouses their torpid powers when Nature fails;
And all these Legendary Tales
Are, to a worn-out mind, Cantharides.

 "But how to cure the evil?" you will say:
"My Recipe is,—laughing it away.

"Lay bare the weak farrago of those men
Who fabricate such visionary schemes,
As if the night-mare rode upon their pen,
And trouble'd all their ink with hideous dreams.

"For instance—when a solemn Ghost stalks in,
And, thro' a mystick tale is busy,
Strip me the Gentleman into his skin—
What is he?

"Truly, ridiculous enough:
Mere trash;—and very childish stuff.

"Draw but a Ghost, or Fiend, of low degree,
And all the bubble's broken!—Let us see."

On a wild Moor, all brown and bleak,
Where broods the heath-frequenting grouse,
There stood a tenement antique;
Lord Hoppergollop's country house.

Here Silence reign'd, with lips of glue,
And undisturb'd maintain'd her law;
Save when the Owl cry'd "whoo! whoo! whoo!"
Or the hoarse Crow croak'd "caw! caw! caw!"

Neglected mansion!—for, 'tis said,
Whene'er the snow came feathering down,
Four barbed steeds,—from the Bull's head,
Carried thy master up to town.

Weak Hoppergollop!—Lords may moan,
Who stake, in London, their estate,
On two, small, rattling, bits of bone;
On little figure, or on great.

Swift whirl the wheels.—He's gone.—A Rose
Remains behind, whose virgin look,
Unseen, must blush in wintry snows,
Sweet, beauteous blossom!—'twas the Cook!

A bolder far than my weak note,
Maid of the Moor! thy charms demand:
Eels might be proud to lose their coat,
If skinn'd by Molly Dumpling's hand.

Long had the fair one sat alone,
Had none remain'd save only she;—
She by herself had been—if one
Had not been left, for company.

'Twas a tall youth, whose cheek's clear hue,
Was tinge'd with health and manly toil;—
Cabbage he sow'd; and, when it grew,
He always cut it off, to boil.

Oft would he cry, "Delve, Delve the hole!
And prune the tree, and trim the root!
And stick the wig upon the pole,
To scare the sparrows from the fruit!"

A small, mute favourite, by day,
Follow'd his step; where'er he wheels

His barrow round the garden gay,
A bob-tail cur is at his heels.

Ah, man! the brute creation see!
Thy constancy oft needs the spur!
While lessons of fidelity
Are found in every bob-tail cur.

Hard toil'd the youth, so fresh and strong,
While Bobtail in his face would look,
And mark'd his master troll the song,—
"Sweet Molly Dumpling! Oh, thou Cook!"

For thus he sung:—while Cupid smile'd;—
Please'd that the Gard'ner own'd his dart,
Which prune'd his passions, running wild,
And grafted true-love on his heart.

Maid of the Moor! his love return!
True love ne'er tints the cheek with shame:
When Gard'ners' hearts, like hot-beds, burn,
A Cook may surely feed the flame.

Ah! not averse from love was she;
Tho' pure as Heaven's snowy flake;
Both love'd: and tho' a Gard'ner he,
He knew not what it was to rake.

Cold blows the blast:—the night's obscure:
The mansion's crazy wainscots crack:
No star appear'd:—and all the Moor,
Like ev'ry other Moor,—was black.

Alone, pale, trembling, near the fire,
The lovely Molly Dumpling sat;
Much did she fear, and much admire
What Thomas Gard'ner could be at.

List'ning, her hand supports her chin;
But, ah! no foot is heard to stir:
He comes not, from the garden, in;
Nor he, nor little bobtail cur.

They cannot come, sweet maid! to thee;
Flesh, both of cur and man, is grass!
And what's impossible can't be;
And never, never, comes to pass!

She paces thro' the hall antique,
To call her Thomas from his toil;
Opes the huge door;—the hinges creak;
Because the hinges wanted oil.

Thrice, on the threshold of the hall,
She "Thomas!" cried, with many a sob;
And thrice on Bobtail did she call,
Exclaiming, sweetly,—"Bob! Bob! Bob!"

Vain maid! a Gard'ner's corpse, 'tis said,
In answers can but ill succeed;
And dogs that hear when they are dead,
Are very cunning Dogs indeed!

Back thro' the hall she bent her way;
All, all was solitude around!
The candle shed a feeble ray,—
Tho' a large mould of four to th' pound.

Full closely to the fire she drew;
Adown her cheek a salt tear stole;
When, lo! a coffin out there flew,
And in her apron burnt a hole!

Spiders their busy death-watch tick'd;
A certain sign that Fate will frown;
The clumsy kitchen clock, too, click'd,
A certain sign it was not down.

More strong and strong her terrors rose;—
Her shadow did the maid appal;—
She tremble'd at her lovely nose,—
It look'd so long against the wall.

Up to her chamber, damp and cold,
She climb'd Lord Hoppergollop's stair;—
Three stories high—long, dull, and old,—
As great Lords' stories often are.

All Nature now appear'd to pause:
And "o'er the one half world seem'd dead;"
No "curtain'd sleep" had she;—because
She had no curtains to her bed.

List'ning she lay;—with iron din,
The clock struck Twelve; the door flew wide;
When Thomas, grimly, glided in,

With little Bobtail by his side.

Tall, like the poplar, was his size,
Green, green his waistcoat was, as leeks;
Red, red as beet-root, were his eyes;
Pale, pale as turnips, were his cheeks!

Soon as the Spectre she espied,
The fear-struck damsel faintly said,
"What wou'd my Thomas?"—he replied,
"Oh! Molly Dumpling! I am dead.

"All in the flower of youth I fell,
Cut off with health's full blossom crown'd;
 I was not ill—but in a well
I tumble'd backwards, and was drown'd.

"Four fathom deep thy love doth lie:
His faithful dog his fate doth share;
We're Fiends;—this is not he and I;
We are not here,—for we are there.

"Yes;—two foul Water-Fiends are we;
Maid of the Moor!—attend us now!
Thy hour's at hand;—we come for thee!"
The little Fiend-Cur said "bow wow!"

"To wind her in her cold, cold grave,
A Holland sheet a maiden likes;
A sheet of water thou shalt have;
Such sheets there are in Holland Dykes."

 The Fiends approach; the Maid did shrink;
Swift thro' the night's foul air they spin;
They took her to the green well's brink,
And, with a souse, they plump'd her in.

So true the fair, so true the youth,
Maids, to this day, their story tell:
And hence the proverb rose, that Truth
Lies in the bottom of a well.

Dick ended:—Tom and Will approve'd his strains;
And thought his Legend made as good a figure
As naturalizing a dull German's brains,
Which beget issues in the Heliconian stews,
Upon a profligate Tenth Muse,
In all the gloomy impotence of vigour.

"'Twas now the very witching time of night,
When Prosers yawn."—Discussion grew diffuse:
Argument's carte and tierce were lost, outright:
And they fought loose.

 Says Will, quite carelessly,—"the other day,
As I was lying on my back,
In bed,
I took a fancy in my head;—
Some writings aren't so difficult as people say;—
They are a knack."

"What writings? whose?" says Tom—raking the cinders.
"Many," cried Will:—"For instance,—Peter Pindar's."
"What! call you his a knack?"—"Yes;—mind his measure,
In that lies half the point that gives us pleasure."
"Pooh!—'tisn't that," Dick cried—
"That has been tried,
 Over and over:—Bless your souls!
'Tis seen in Crazy Tales, and twenty things beside:
His measure is as old as Poles."

"Granted," cries Will: "I know I'm speaking treason:
For Peter,
With many a joke, and queer conceit, doth season
His metre:

"And this I'll say of Peter, to his face,
As 'twas, time past, of Vanbrugh writ—
Peter has often wanted grace,
But he has never wanted wit.

"Yet I will tell you a plain tale,
And see how far quaint measure will prevail:"

THE NEWCASTLE APOTHECARY

A man, in many a country town, we know,
Professes openly with death to wrestle;
Ent'ring the field against the grimly foe,
Arm'd with a mortar and a pestle.

Yet, some affirm, no enemies they are;
But meet just like prize-fighters, in a Fair,
 Who first shake hands before they box,

Then give each other plaguy knocks,
With all the love and kindness of a brother:
So (many a suff'ring Patient saith)
Tho' the Apothecary fights with Death,
Still they're sworn friends to one another.

A member of this Æsculapian line,
Lived at Newcastle upon Tyne:
No man could better gild a pill:
Or make a bill;
Or mix a draught, or bleed, or blister;
Or draw a tooth out of your head;
Or chatter scandal by your bed;
Or give a clyster.

Of occupations these were quantum suff.:
Yet, still, he thought the list not long enough;
And therefore Midwifery he chose to pin to't.
 This balance'd things:—for if he hurl'd
A few score mortals from the world,
He made amends by bringing others into't.

His fame full six miles round the country ran;
In short, in reputation he was solus:
All the old women call'd him "a fine man!"
His name was Bolus.

Benjamin Bolus, tho' in trade,
(Which oftentimes will Genius fetter)
Read works of fancy, it is said;
And cultivated the Belles Lettres.

And why should this be thought so odd?
Can't men have taste who cure a phthysic;
Of Poetry tho' Patron-God,
Apollo patronises physick.
 Bolus love'd verse;—and took so much delight in't,
That his prescriptions he resolve'd to write in't.

No opportunity he e'er let pass
Of writing the directions, on his labels,
In dapper couplets,—like Gay's Fables;
Or, rather, like the lines in Hudibras.

Apothecary's verse!—and where's the treason?
'Tis simply honest dealing:—not a crime;—
When patients swallow physick without reason,
It is but fair to give a little rhyme.

He had a Patient lying at death's door,
Some three miles from the town,—it might be four;
To whom, one evening, Bolus sent an article,
In Pharmacy, that's call'd cathartical.

And, on the label of the stuff,
He wrote this verse;
Which, one would think, was clear enough,
And terse:—

"When taken,
To be well shaken."

Next morning, early, Bolus rose;
And to the Patient's house he goes;—
Upon his pad,
Who a vile trick of stumbling had:
It was, indeed, a very sorry hack;
But that's of course:
For what's expected from a horse
With an Apothecary on his back?
Bolus arrive'd; and gave a doubtful tap;—
Between a single and a double rap.—

Knocks of this kind
Are given by Gentlemen who teach to dance:
By Fiddlers, and by Opera-singers:
One loud, and then a little one behind;
As if the knocker fell, by chance,
Out of their fingers.

The Servant lets him in, with dismal face,
Long as a courtier's out of place—
Portending some disaster;
John's countenance as rueful look'd, and grim,
As if th' Apothecary had physick'd him,—
And not his master.

"Well, how's the Patient?" Bolus said:—
John shook his head.
"Indeed!—hum! ha!—that's very odd!
He took the draught?"—John gave a nod.
"Well,—how?—what then?—speak out, you dunce!"
"Why then"—says John—"we shook him once."
"Shook him!—how?"—Bolus stammer'd out:
"We jolted him about."
"Zounds! Shake a Patient, man!—a shake won't do."

"No, Sir,—and so we gave him two."
"Two shakes! od's curse!
'Twould make the Patient worse."
"It did so, Sir!—and so a third we tried."
"Well, and what then?"—"then, Sir, my master died."

Vignette of a mortar and pestle sitting atop a draped casket.

 Ere Will had done 'twas waxing wond'rous late;
And reeling Bucks the streets began to scour;
While guardian Watchmen, with a tottering gait,
Cried every thing, quite clear, except the hour.

"Another pot," says Tom, "and then,
A Song;—and so good night, good Gentlemen!

"I've Lyricks, such as Bons Vivants indite,
In which your bibbers of Champagne delight,—
The Poetaster, bawling them in clubs,
Obtains a miserably noted name;
And every noisy Bacchanalian dubs
The Singing-Writer with a bastard Fame."

LODGINGS FOR SINGLE GENTLEMEN

Who has e'er been in London, that overgrown place,
Has seen "Lodgings to Let" stare him full in the face:
Some are good, and let dearly; while some, 'tis well known,
Are so dear, and so bad, they are best let alone.

 WILL WADDLE, whose temper was studious and lonely,
Hire'd lodgings that took Single Gentlemen only;
But Will was so fat he appear'd like a ton;—
Or like Two Single Gentlemen roll'd into One.

He enter'd his rooms, and to bed he retreated;
But, all the night long, he felt fever'd, and heated;
And, tho' heavy to weigh, as a score of fat sheep,
He was not, by any means, heavy to sleep.

Next night 'twas the same!—and the next;—and the next;
He perspire'd like an ox; he was nervous, and vex'd;
Week past after week; till, by weekly succession,
His weakly condition was past all expression.

In six months, his acquaintance began much to doubt him:

For his skin, "like a lady's loose gown," hung about him.
He sent for a Doctor; and cried, like a ninny,
"I have lost many pounds—make me well—there's a guinea."

The Doctor look'd wise:—"a slow fever," he said:
Prescribe'd sudorificks,—and going to bed.
"Sudorificks in bed," exclaim'd Will, "are humbugs!
I've enough of them there, without paying for drugs!"

Will kick'd out the Doctor:—but, when ill indeed,
E'en dismissing the Doctor don't always succeed;
So, calling his host—he said—"Sir, do you know,
I'm the fat Single Gentleman, six months ago?

"Look'e, landlord, I think," argued Will, with a grin,
"That with honest intentions you first took me in:
But from the first night—and to say it I'm bold—
I have been so damn'd hot, that I'm sure I caught cold."

Quoth the landlord—"till now, I ne'er had a dispute;
I've let lodgings ten years;—I'm a Baker, to boot;
In airing your sheets, Sir, my wife is no sloven;
And your bed is immediately over my Oven."

"The Oven!!!" says Will;—says the host, "why this passion?
In that excellent bed died three people of fashion.
Why so crusty, good Sir?"—"Zounds!" cries Will, in a taking,
"Who wouldn't be crusty, with half a year's baking?"

Will paid for his rooms;—cried the host, with a sneer,
"Well, I see you've been going away half a year:"
"Friend, we can't well agree,—yet no quarrel"—Will said;—
"But I'd rather not perish, while you make your bread."2
A melting candle sits on a bread peel in front of a brick oven.

THE KNIGHT AND THE FRIAR

PART FIRST

In our Fifth Harry's reign, when 'twas the fashion
To thump the French, poor creatures! to excess;—
Tho' Britons, now a days, shew more compassion,
And thump them, certainly, a great deal less;—

In Harry's reign, when flush'd Lancastrian roses
Of York's pale blossoms had usurp'd the right;3

As wine drives Nature out of drunkards' noses,
Till red, triumphantly, eclipses white;—
In Harry's reign—but let me to my song,
Or good king Harry's reign may seem too long.

Sir Thomas Erpingham, a gallant knight,
When this king Harry went to war, in France,
Girded a sword about his middle;
Resolving, very lustily, to fight,
And teach the Frenchmen how to dance,
Without a fiddle.

 And wond'rous bold Sir Thomas prove'd in battle,
Performing prodigies, with spear and shield;
His valour, like a murrain among cattle,
Was reckon'd very fatal in the field.
Yet, tho' Sir Thomas had an iron fist,
He was, at heart, a mild Philanthropist.

Much did he grieve, when making Frenchmen die,
To any inconvenience to put 'em:
"It quite distress'd his feelings," he would cry,
"That he must cut their throats,"—and, then he cut 'em.

Thus, during many a Campaign,
He cut, and grieve'd, and cut, and came again;—
Pitying, and killing;—
 Lamenting sorely for men's souls,
While pretty little eyelet holes,
Clean thro' their bodies he kept drilling:

Till palling on his Laurels, grown so thick,
(As boys pull blackberries, till they are sick,)
Homeward he bent his course, to wreath 'em;
And in his Castle, near fair Norwich town,
Glutted with glory, he sat down,
In perfect solitude, beneath 'em.

Now, sitting under Laurels, Heroes say,
Gives grace, and dignity—and so it may—
When men have done campaigning;
But, certainly, these gentlemen must own
That sitting under Laurels, quite alone,
Is much more dignified than entertaining.

 Pious Æneas, who, in his narration
Of his own prowess, felt so great a charm;—
(For, tho' he feign'd great grief in the relation,

He made the story longer than your arm;)

Pious Æneas no more pleasure knew
Than did our Knight—who could he pious too—
In telling his exploits, and martial brawls:
But pious Thomas had no Dido near him—
No Queen—King, Lord, nor Commoner to hear him—
So he was force'd to tell them to the walls:
 And to his Castle walls, in solemn guise,
The knight, full often, did soliloquize:—

For "Walls have ears," Sir Thomas had been told;
Yet thought the tedious hours would seem much shorter,
If, now and then, a tale he could unfold
To ears of flesh and blood, not stone and mortar.

At length, his old Castellum grew so dull,
That legions of Blue Devils seize'd the Knight;
Megrim invested his belaurell'd skull;
Spleen laid embargoes on his appetite;

 Till, thro' the day-time, he was haunted, wholly,
By all the imps of "loathed Melancholy!"—
Heaven keep her, and her imps, for ever, from us!—
An Incubus, whene'er he went to bed,
Sat on his stomach, like a lump of lead,
Making unseemly faces at Sir Thomas.

Plagues such as these might make a Parson swear;
Sir Thomas being but a Layman,
Swore, very roundly, à la militaire,
Or, rather, (from vexation) like a Drayman:

 Damning his Walls, out of all line and level;
Sinking his drawbridges and moats;
Wishing that he were cutting throats—
And they were at the devil.

"What's to be done," Sir Thomas said one day,
"To drive Ennui away?
How is the evil to be parried?
What can remind me of my former life?—
Those happy days I spent in noise and strife!"
The last word struck him;—"Zounds!" says he,
"a Wife!"—
And so he married.

Muse! regulate your pace;—

Restrain, awhile, your frisking, and your giggling!
Here is a stately Lady in the case:
We mustn't, now, be fidgetting, and niggling.

 O God of Love! Urchin of spite, and play!
Deserter, oft, from saffron Hymen's quarters;
His torch bedimming, as thou runn'st away,
Till half his Votaries become his Martyrs!

Sly, wandering God! whose frolick arrows pass
Thro' hearts of Potentates, and Prentice-boys;
Who mark'st with Milkmaids' forms, the tell-tale grass,
And make'st the fruitful Prude repent her joys!

Drop me one feather, from thy wanton wing,
Young God of dimples! in thy roguish flight;
And let thy Poet catch it, now, to sing
The beauty of the Dame who won the Knight!

Her beauty!—but Sir Thomas's own Sonnet
Beats all that I can say upon it.

SIR THOMAS ERPINGHAM'S SONNET ON HIS LADY

I
Such star-like lustre lights her Eyes,
They must have darted from a Sphere,
Our duller System to surprise,
Outshining all the Planets here;
 And, having wander'd from their wonted place,
Fix in the wond'rous Heaven of her Face.

II
The modest Rose, whose blushes speak
The ardent kisses of the Sun,
Off'ring a tribute to her Cheek,
Droops, to perceive its Tint outdone;
Then withering with envy and despair,
Dies on her Lips, and leaves its Fragrance there.

III
Ringlets, that to her Breast descend,
Increase the beauties they invade;
Thus branches in luxuriance bend,
To grace the lovely Hills they shade;
And thus the glowing Climate did entice

Tendrils to curl, unprune'd, o'er Paradise.

Sir Thomas having close'd his love-sick strain,
Come, buxom Muse! and let us frisk again!

Close to a Chapel, near the Castle-gates,
Dwelt certain stickers in the Devil's skirts;
Who, with prodigious fervour, shave their pates,
And shew a most religious scorn for shirts.

Their House's sole Endowment was our Knight's:—
Thither an Abbot, and twelve Friars, retreating,
Conquer'd (sage, pious men!) their appetites
With that infallible specifick—eating.

'Twould seem, since tenanted by holy Friars,
That Peace and Harmony reign'd here eternally;—
Whoever told you so were cursed liars;—
The holy Friars quarrell'd most infernally.

Not a day past
Without some schism among these heavenly lodgers;
But none of their dissensions seem'd to last
So long as Friar John's and Friar Roger's.

I have been very accurate in my researches,
And find this Convent (truce with whys and hows)
Kept in a constant ferment with the rows
Of these two quarrelsome fat sons of Churches.

But when Sir Thomas went to his devotions,
Proceeding thro' their Cloister with his Bride,
You never could have dream'd of their commotions,
The stiff-rump'd rascals look'd so sanctified:

And it became the custom of the Knight
To go to matins every day;
He jogg'd his Bride, as soon as it was light,
Crying, "my dear, 'tis time for us to pray."—

This custom he establish'd, very soon,
After his honey-moon.

Wives of this age might think his zeal surprising;
But much his pious lady did it please,
To see her Husband, every morning, rising,
And going, instantly, upon his knees.

Never, I ween,
In any person's recollection,
Was such a couple seen,
For genuflection!

Making as great a drudgery of prayer
As humble Curates are oblige'd to do,—
Whose labour, wo the while! scarce buys them cassocks;

And, every morning, whether foul or fair,
Sir Thomas and the Dame were in their pew,
Craw-thumping, upon hassocks.

It could not otherwise befall
(Sir Thomas, and his Wife, this course pursuing,)
But that the Lady, affable to all,
 Should greet the Friars, on her way
To matins, as she met them, every day,
Good morninging, and how d'ye doing:

Now nodding to this Friar, now to that,
As thro' the Cloister she was wont to trip;
Stopping, sometimes, to have a little chat,
On casual topicks, with the holy brothers;—
So condescending was her Ladyship,
To Roger, John, and all the others.

All this was natural enough
To any female of urbanity;—
But holy men are made of as frail stuff
As all the lighter sons of Vanity!—

 And these her Ladyship's chaste condescensions,
In Friar John bred damnable desire;
Heterodox, unclean intentions;—
Abominable in a Friar!

Whene'er she greeted him, his gills grew red,
While she was quite unconscious of the matter;—
But he, the beast! was casting sheeps-eyes at her,
Out of his bullock-head.

That coxcombs were and are, I need not give,
Nor take the trouble, now, to prove;
Nor that those dead, like many, now, who live,
Have thought a Lady's condescension, love.

This happen'd with fat Friar John!—

Monastick Coxcomb! amorous, and gummy;
Fill'd with conceit up to his very brim!—
He thought his guts and garbage doated on,
By a fair Dame, whose Husband was to him
Hyperion to a mummy.

Burning with flames the Lady never knew,
Hotter and heavier than toasted cheese,
He sent her a much warmer billet-doux
Than Abelard e'er writ to Eloïse.

But whether Friar John's fat shape and face,
Tho' pleading both together,
 Were sorry advocates, in such a case;—
Or, whether
He marr'd his hopes, by suffering his pen
With too much fervour to display 'em;—
As very tender Nurses, now and then,
Cuddle their Children, till they overlay 'em;—

'Twas plain, his pray'r to decorate the brows
Of good Sir Thomas was so far from granted,
That the Dame went, directly, to her spouse,
And told him what the filthy Friar wanted.

Think, Reader, think! if thou hast ta'en, for life,
A partner to thy bed, for worse or better,
 Think what Sir Thomas felt, when his chaste wife
Brandish'd, before his eyes, the Friar's letter!

He felt, Sir,—Zounds!—
Yes, Zounds! I say, Sir,—for it makes me swear—
More torture than he suffer'd from the wounds
 He got among the French, in France;—
Not that I take upon me to advance
The knight was ever wounded there.

Think gravely, Sir, I pray:—fancy the Knight—
('Tis quite a Picture)—with his heart's delight!
Fancy you see his virtuous Lady stand,
Holding the Friar's foulness in her hand!—

How should Sir Thomas, Sir, behave?
Why bounce, and sputter, surely, like a squib:—
You would have done the same, Sir, if a knave,
A frouzy Friar, meddle'd with your Rib.

His bosom almost burst with ire

Against the Friar;
 Rage gave his face an apoplectick hue;
His cheeks turn'd purple, and his nose turn'd blue;
He swore with this mock Saint he'd soon be even;—
He'd have him flay'd, like Saint Bartholomew;—
And, now again, he'd have him stone'd, like Stephen.

But, "Ira furor brevis est,"
As Horace, quaintly, has express'd;—

Therefore the Knight, finding his foam and froth
Work thro' the bung-hole of his mouth, like beer,
Pull'd out the vent-peg of his wrath,
To let the stream of his revenge run clear:

Debating, with himself, what mode might suit him,
To trounce the rogue who wanted to cornute him.
 First, an attack against his Foe he plann'd,
Learn'd in the Field, where late he fought so felly;
That is—to march up, bravely, sword in hand,
And run the Friar thro' his holy belly.

At last, his better judgment did declare—
Seeing his honour would as little shine
By sticking Friars, as by killing swine—
To circumvent him, by a ruse de guerre:

And, as the project ripen'd in his head,
Thus to his virtuous Wife he said:—

"Now sit thee down, my Lady bright!
And list thy Lord's desire;
An assignation thou shalt write,
Beshrew me! to the Friar.

 "Aread him, at the midnight hour,
In silent sort to go,
And bide thy coming, in the Bower—
For there do Crabsticks grow.

"He shall not tarry long;—for why?
When Twelve have striking done,
Then, by the God of Gardens! I
Will cudgel him till One."

 The Lady wrote just what Sir Thomas told her;
For, it is no less strange than true,
That Wives did, once, what Husbands bid them do;—

Lord! how this World improves, as we grow older!

She name'd the midnight hour;—
Telling the Friar to repair
To the sweet, secret Bower;—
But not a word of any crabsticks there.

Thus have I seen a liquorish, black rat,
Lure'd by the Cook, to sniff, and smell her bacon;
And, when he's eager for a bit of fat,
Down goes a trap upon him, and he's taken.

A tiny Page,—for, formerly, a boy
Was a mere dunce who did not understand
The doctrines of Sir Pandarus, of Troy,—
Slipp'd the Dame's note into the Friar's hand,
As he was walking in the cloister;
And, then, slipp'd off,—as silent as an oyster.

The Friar read;—the Friar chuckle'd:—
For, now the Farce's unities were right:
Videlicet—The Argument, a Cuckold;
The Scene, a Bow'r; Time, Twelve o'clock, at night.

Blithe was fat John!—and, dreading no mishap,
Stole, at the hour appointed, to the trap;
But, so perfume'd, so musk'd, for the occasion,—
His tribute to the nose so like invasion,—
You would have sworn, to smell him, 'twas no rat,
But a dead, putrified, old civet-cat.

He reach'd the spot, anticipating blisses,
Soft murmurs, melting sighs, and burning kisses,
Trances of joy, and mingling of the souls;
When, whack! Sir Thomas hit him on the jowls.

Now, on his head it came, now on his face,
His neck, and shoulders, arms, legs, breast, and back;
In short, on almost every place
We read of in the Almanack.

Blows rattle'd on him thick as hail;
Making him rue the day that he was born;—
Sir Thomas plied his cudgel like a flail,
And thrash'd as if he had been thrashing corn.

At length, a thump,—(painful the facts, alas!
Truth urges us Historians to relate!)—

Took Friar John so smart athwart the pate,
It acted like a perfect coup de grace.

Whether it was a random shot,
Or aim'd maliciously,—tho' Fame says not—
Certain his soul (the Knight so crack'd his crown)
Fled from his body; but which way it went,
Or whether Friars' souls fly up, or down,
Remains a matter of nice argument.

 Points so abstruse I dare not dwell upon;
Enough, for me, his body is not gone;—

For I have business, still, in my narration,
With the fat carcass of this holy porpus;
And Death, tho' sharp in his Administration,
Never suspended such an Habeas Corpus.

THE KNIGHT AND THE FRIAR

PART THE SECOND

Reader! if you have Genius, you'll discover,
Do what you will to keep it cool,
It, now and then, in spite of you, boils over,
Upon a fool.

 Haven't you (lucky man if not) been vex'd,
Worn, fretted, and perplex'd,
By a pert, busy, would-be-clever knave,
A forward, empty, self-sufficient slave?

And haven't you, all christian patience gone,
At last, put down the puppy with your wit;—
On whom it seem'd, tho' you had Mines of it,
Extravagance to spend a jest upon?—

And haven't you, (I'm sure you have, my friend!)
When you have laid the puppy low,—
All little pique, and malice, at an end,—
Been sorry for the blow?
And said, (if witty, so would say your Bard,)
"Damn it! I hit that meddling fool too hard?"

Thus did the brave Sir Thomas say;—
Whose Genius didn't much disturb his pate:

It rather, in his bones, and muscles, lay,—
Like many other men's of good estate:

Thus did Sir Thomas say;—and well he might,
When pity to resentment did succeed;
For, certainly, (tho' not with wit) the Knight
Had hit the Friar very hard, indeed!
And heads, nineteen in twenty, 'tis confest,
Can feel a crab-stick sooner than a jest.

There was, in the Knight's family, a man
Cast in the roughest mould Dame Nature boasts;
With shoulders wider than a dripping pan,
And legs as thick, about the calves, as posts.

 All the domesticks, viewing, in this hulk,
So large a specimen of Nature's whims,
With kitchen wit, allusive to his bulk,
Had christen'd him the Duke of Limbs.

Thro'out the Castle, every whipper-snapper
Was canvassing the merits of this strapper:
Most of the Men voted his size alarming;
But all the Maids, nem. con. declare'd it charming!

This wight possess'd a quality most rare;—
I tremble when I mention it, I swear!
Lest pretty Ladies question my veracity:
'Twas—when he had a secret in his care,
To keep it, with the greatest pertinacity.

 Pour but a secret in him, and 'twould glue him
Like rosin, on a well-cork'd bottle's snout;
Had twenty devils come with cork-screws to him,
They never could have screw'd the secret out.

Now, when Sir Thomas, in the dark, alone,
Had kill'd a Friar, weighing twenty stone,
Whose carcass must be hid, before the dawn,
Judging he might as hopelessly desire
To move a Convent as the Friar,

He thought on this man's secresy, and brawn;—
And, like a swallow, o'er the lawn he skims,
Up to the Cock-loft of the Duke of Limbs:
 Where Somnus, son of Nox, the humble copy
Of his own daughter Mors,8 had made assault
On the Duke's eye-lids,—not with juice of poppy,

But potent draughts, distill'd from hops and malt.

Certainly, nothing operates much quicker
Against two persons' secret dialogues,
Than one of them being asleep, in liquor,
Snoring like twenty thousand hogs.

 Yet circumstance did, pressingly, require
The Knight to tell his tale;
And to instruct his Man, knock'd down with ale,
That he (Sir Thomas) had knock'd down a Friar.

How wake a man, in such a case?
Sir, the best method—I have tried a score—
Is, when his nose is playing thoro' bass,
To pull it, till you make him roar.

A Sleeper's nose is made on the same plan
As the small wire 'twixt a Doll's wooden thighs;
For pull the nose, or wire, the Doll, or Man,
Will open, in a minute, both their eyes.

 This mode Sir Thomas took,—and, in a trice,
Grasp'd, with his thumb and finger, like a vice,
That feature which the human face embosses,
And pull'd the Duke of Limbs by the proboscis.

The Man awoke, and goggle'd on his master;—
He saw his Master goggling upon him;—
Fresh from concluding, on a Friar's nob,
What Coroners would call an awkward job,
He glare'd, all horror-struck and grim,—
Paler than Paris-plaister!

His hair stuck up, like bristles on a pig;—
So Garrick look'd, when he perform'd Macbeth;
Who, ere he entered, after Duncan's death,
Rumple'd his wig.

 The Knight cried, "Follow me!"—with strange grimaces;
The Man arose,—
And began "sacrificing to the Graces,"
By putting on his clothes;

But he reverse'd, in making himself smart,
A Scotchman's toilet, altogether:
And merely clapp'd a cover on that part
The Highlanders expose to wind and weather.

They reach'd the bower where the Friar lay;
When, to his Man,
The Knight began,
In doleful accents, thus to say:

"Here a fat Friar lies, kill'd with a mauling,
For coming, in the dark, a-caterwauling;
Whom I (O cursed spite!) did lay so!"
Thus, solemnly, Sir Thomas spake, and sigh'd;—
To whom the Duke of Limbs replied—
"Odrabbit it! Sir Thomas! you don't say so!"

Then, taking the huge Friar per the hocks,
He whirl'd the ton of blubber three times round,
And swung it on his shoulders, from the ground,
 With strength that yields, in any age, to no man's,—
Tho' Milo's ghost should rise, bearing the Ox
He carried at the games of the old Romans.

Nay, I opine—let Fame say what it can—
Of ancient vigour, (Fame is, oft, a Liar)
That Milo was a pigmy to this Man,
And his fat Ox quite skinny to the Friar.

Besides,—I hold it in much doubt
If Roman graziers (should the truth come out)
Were, like the English, knowing in the matter;—
—I wouldn't breed my beast more Romano;—

 For, I suspect, in fatt'ning they were dull,
And when they made an ox out of a bull,
They fed him ill,—and, then, he got no fatter
Than a fat opera Soprano.

Over the moat, (the draw-bridge being down)
Gallantly stalk'd the brawny Duke of Limbs,
Bearing Johannes, of the shaven crown,
Fame'd, when alive, for spoiling maids, and hymns;
For mangling Pater-Nosters, and goose-pies,
And telling sundry beads,—and sundry lies.

 Across a marsh he strode, with steadier gait
Than Satan trod the Syrtis, at his fall,
And perch'd himself, with his monastick weight,
Upon the Convent-garden's wall;—

Whence, on the grounds within it, as he gaze'd,

To find a spot where he might leave his load,
He 'spied a House so little, it seem'd raise'd
More for Man's visits, than his fix'd abode;—
And Cynthia aided him to gaze his fill,
For, now, she sought Endymion on the hill.

Arise, Tarquinius! shew thy lofty face!
While I describe, with dignity, the place.
 Snug in an English garden's shadiest spot,
A structure stands, and welcomes many a breeze;
Lonely, and simple as a Ploughman's cot,
Where Monarchs may unbend, who wish for ease.

There sit Philosophers; and sitting read;
And to some end apply the dullest pages;
And pity the Barbarians, north of Tweed,
Who scout these fabricks of the southern Sages.

Sure, for an Edifice in estimation,
Never was any less presuming seen!
It shrinks, so modestly, from observation!
And hides behind all sorts of evergreen;—
Like a coy Maid, design'd for filthy Man,
Peeping, at his approach, behind her fan.

 Into this place, unnotice'd by beholders,
The Duke of Limbs, most circumspectly, stole,
And shot the Friar off his shoulders,
Just like a sack of round Newcastle coal:

Not taking any pains,
Nor caring, in the least,
How he deposited the Friar's remains,
No more than if a Friar were a beast.

No funeral, of which you ever heard,
Was mark'd with ceremonies half so slight;
For John was left, not like the dead interr'd,
But, like the living, sitting bolt upright!

 Has no shrewd Reader, of one sex or t'other,
Recurring to the facts already stated,
Thought on a certain Roger?—that same brother
Who hated John, and whom John hated?

'Tis, now, a necessary thing to say
That, at this juncture, Roger wasn't well;
Poor Man! he had been rubbing, all the day,

His stomach with coarse towels:
And clapping trenchers, hot as hell,
Upon his bowels;
Where spasms were kicking up a furious frolick,
Afflicting him with mulligrubs and cholick.

He also had imbibe'd, to sooth his pains,
Of pulvis rhei very many grains;
 And to the garden's deepest shade was bent,
To give, quite privily, his sorrows vent:

When, there,—alive and merry to appearance—
He 'spied his ancient foe, by the moon's light!—
Who sat erect, with so much perseverance,
It look'd as if he kept his post in spite.

A case it is of piteous distress,
If, carrying a secret grief about,
We wish to bury it in a recess,
And find another there, who keeps us out.

Expecting, soon, his enemy to go,
Roger, at first, walk'd to and fro,
 With tolerably tranquil paces;
But finding John determine'd to remain,
Roger, each time he pass'd, thro' spite or pain,
Made, at his adversary, hideous faces.

How misery will lower human pride!
And make us buckle!—
Roger, who, all his life, had John defied,
Was now oblige'd to speak him fair,—and truckle.

"Behold me," Roger cried, "behold me, John!
Entreating as a favour you'll be gone;
Me! your sworn foe, tho' fellow-lodger;
Me!—who, in agony, tho' suing now to you,
Would, once, have seen you damn'd ere make a bow to you.
Me,—Roger!"

 To this address, so fraught with the pathetick,
John remain'd dumb, as a Pythagorean;
Seeming to hint, "Roger, you're a plebeian
Peripatetick."

When such choice oratory has not hit,
When it is, e'en, unanswer'd by a grunt,
'Twould justify tame Job to curse a bit,

And set an Angler swearing, in his punt.

Cholerick Roger could not brook it;—
So seeing a huge brick-bat, up he took it;
 And aiming, like a marksman at a crow,
Plump on the breast he hit his deadly foe;
Who fell, like Pedants' periods, to the ground,—
Very inanimate, and very round.

Here is another Picture, reader mine!
I gave you one in the first Canto;—
This is more solemn, mystical, and fine,—
Like something in the Castle of Otranto.

Bring, bring me, now, a Painter, for the work,
Who on the subject will, with furor, rush!
Some Artist who can sup upon raw pork,
To make him dream of horrors, for his brush!

 Come, Limners, come! who choke your house's entry
With dear, unmeaning lumber, from your easels;
Dull heads of the Nobility and Gentry;
Full length of fubsey Belles, or Beaux like weasels!

Come, Limners, hither come! and draw
A finer incident than e'er ye saw!
Here is a John, by moon-light, (a fat monk)
Lying stone dead; and, here, a Roger, quick!

And over John stands Roger, in a funk,
Supposing he has kill'd him with a brick!
There, Painters! there!
Now, by Apelles's gamboge, I swear!

 Such a dead subject never comes,
Among those lifeless living ye display;
Then, thro' your palettes thrust your graphick thumbs,—
And work away!

Seeing John dead as a door nail,
Roger began to wring his hands, and wail;
Calling himself, Beast, Butcher, cruel Turk!
Thrice "Benedicite!" he mutter'd;
Thrice, in the eloquence of grief he utter'd;
"I've done a pretty job of journey-work!"

Some people will shew symptoms of repentance
When Conscience, like a chastening Angel, smites 'em;

Some from mere dread of the Law's sentence,
When Newgate, like the very Devil, frights 'em;—

That Virtue's struggles, in the heart, denotes,
This Vice's hints, to men's left ears, and throats.

Now Roger's conscience, it appears,
Was not, by half, so lively as his fears.

His breast, soon after he was born,
Grew like an Hostler's lantern, at an Inn;—
All the circumference was dirty horn,
And feebly blink'd the ray of warmth within.

In short, for one of his religious function,
His Conscience was both cowardly and callous;
No melting Cherub whisper'd to't "Compunction!"
But grim Jack Ketch disturb'd it, crying "Gallows!"
And all his sorrow, for this deed abhorr'd,
Was nothing but antipathy to cord.

A padlock'd door stood in the garden wall,
Where John, by Roger's brick-bat, chance'd to fall,
And Roger had a key that could undo it;
Thro' this same door, at any time of day,
They brought, into the Convent, corn, and hay;—
Sometimes, at dusk, a pretty girl came thro' it:
Just to confess herself, to some grave codger;
Perhaps, she came to John,—perhaps, to Roger.

Out at this portal Roger made a shift
To lug his worst of foes:
For, seizing (as the gout was wont) his toes,
He dragg'd the load he couldn't lift.

Achilles, thus, drew round the Trojan plain,
The ten years' Adversary he had slain.—

Yet,—for I scorn a Grecian to disparage,—
Achilles in more style, and splendour, did it;
He sported Murder strapp'd behind his carriage,—
But bourgeois Roger sneak'd on foot, and hid it.

Roger, however, labour'd on,—
Puffing and tugging;—
And hauling John,
As fishermen, on shore, haul up a boat;
Till, after a great deal of lugging,

He lugg'd him to the edge of the Knight's moat;
 And stuck him up so straight upon his rear,
Touching, almost, the water, with his heels,
That the defunct might pass, not seen too near,
For some fat gentleman who bobb'd for eels.

Swiftly did Roger, then, retrace his ground,
Lighter than he came out, by many a pound.

So have I seen, on Marlb'rough downs, a hack,
Ease'd of a great man's chaise, and coming back,
From Bladud's springs, upon the western road;
No bloated Noble's luggage at his rump,
Whose doom's, that dread of pick-pockets, the pump,
He canters home, from Bath, without his load.

 Sir Thomas being scrupulous, and queasy,
Couldn't, in all this interval, be easy.

He went to bed;—and, there, began to burn;
Nine times he turn'd, in wondrous perturbation;—
He woke her Ladyship, at every turn,
And gave her, full nine times, complete vexation.

To seek the Duke of Limbs, at length, he rose,
And prowl'd with him, lamenting Fortune's stripes;
Now in the rookery among the crows,
Now squashing in the marsh, among the snipes:

Wishing strange wishes;—among many,
He wish'd—ere he had clapp'd his eyes on any.
 All Priests, and Crabsticks, thrown into the fire;—
Or, seeing Providence ordain'd it so,
That Priest, and Crabstick, (to his grief) must grow,
He wish'd stout Crabstick couldn't kill fat Friar.

Men's wishes will be partial, now and then;—
As, in this case, 'tis plainly seen;
Wherein, Sir Thomas, full of spleen,
Wish'd to burn all the Crabs, and Clergymen.

Think ye that he,—at wishing tho' a dab,—
To wish such harm to any Knight would urge ye?
Yet he, a Knight, had taken up a Crab,
And thump'd to death, with it, one of the Clergy.

 As he went wishing on,
With the great Duke of Limbs behind him,—

Horror on horror!—he saw John
Where least of all he ever thought to find him:

Stuck up, on end, in placid grace,
Like a stuff'd Kangaroo,—tho' vastly fatter,—
With the full moon upon his chubby face,
Like a brass pot-lid shining on a platter.

"'Sdeath!" quoth the Knight, of half his powers bereft,
"Didst thou not tell me where this Friar was left?
Men rise again, to push us from our stools!"
To which the Duke replied, with steady phiz,—
 "Them as took pains to push that Friar from his,
At such a time o'night, was cursed fools."

"Ah!" sigh'd Sir Thomas, "while I wander here,
By fortune stamp'd a Homicide, alas!"
(And, as he spoke, a penitential tear
Mingled with Heaven's dew-drops, on the grass;)—
"Will no one from my eyes yon Spectre pull?"
"Sir Thomas," said the Duke of Limbs, "I wool."

He would have thrown the garbage in the moat,
But the Knight told him fat was prone to float.

The Lout, at length, having bethought him,
Heave'd up the Friar on his back once more;
And (Castles having armories of yore)
Into the Knight's old Armory he brought him.

 Among the gorgeous, shining Coats of Mail,
That grace'd the walls, on high, in gallant shew,—
As pewter pots, in houses fame'd for ale,
Glitter, above the Bar-maid, in a row,—

A curious, antique suit was hoarded,
Cover'd with dust;
Which had, for many years, afforded
An iron dinner to that ostrich, Rust.

Though this was all too little,—in a minute,
The Duke of Limbs ramm'd the fat Friar in it;
So a good Housewife takes a narrow skin,
To make black puddings, and stuffs hog's meat in.

 The Knight, who saw this ceremony pass,
Inquire'd the meaning; when the Duke did say,—
"I'll tie him on ould Dumpling, that's at grass,

And turn him out, a top of the highway."

This Steed,—who now, it seems, was grazing,—
In the French wars had often borne the Knight;—
His symmetry beyond the power of praising,
And prouder than Bucephalus, in fight!

Once, how he paw'd the ground, and snuff'd the gale!
Uncropp'd his ears, undock'd his flowing tail;
No blemish was within him, nor without him;
Perfect he was in every part;—
No barbarous Farrier, with infernal art,
Had mutilated the least bit about him.

Of high Arabian pedigree,
Father of many four-foot babes was he;
And sweet hoof'd Beauties still would he be rumpling;
But, counting five and twenty from his birth,
At grass for life, unwieldy in the girth,
He had obtain'd, alas! the name of Dumpling.

Now, at the postern stood the gay old Charger;
Saddle'd, and house'd,—in full caparison!—
Now on his back,—no rider larger,—
Upright, and stiff, and tied with cords, sat John:
Arm'd cap-à-pié completely, like a knight
Going to fight.

A Lance was in the rest, of stately beech:
Nothing was wanting, but a Page, or 'Squire;—
The Duke, with thistles, switch'd old Dumpling's breech;
And off he clatter'd with the martial Friar.
Now, in the Convent let us take a peep,—
Where Roger, like Sir Thomas, couldn't sleep:

Instead of singing requiems, and psalms,
For fat John's soul, he had been seize'd with qualms,
Thinking it would be rash to tarry there;—
And having, prudently, resolve'd on flight,
Knock'd up a neighbouring miller, in the night,
And borrow'd his grey Mare.

Thus, trotting off,—beneath a row of trees
He saw "a sight that made his marrow freeze!"
A furious Warrior follow'd him, in mail,
Upon a Charger, close at his Mare's tail!

He cross'd himself!—and, canting, cried,

Oh, sadly have I sinned!
Then stuck his heels in his Mare's side;
And, then, old Dumpling whinny'd!

Roger whipp'd, and Roger spurr'd,
Distilling drops of fear!
But while he spurr'd, still, still he heard
The wanton Dumpling at his rear.

'Twas dawn!—he look'd behind him, in the chase;
When, lo! the features of fat John,—
His beaver up, and pressing on,—
Glare'd, ghastly, in the wretched Roger's face!

The Miller's Mare, who oft had gone the way,
Scamper'd with Roger into Norwich town;
And, there, to all the market-folks' dismay,
Old Dumpling beat the mare, with Roger, down.

Brief let me be;—the Story soon took air;—
For Townsmen are inquisitive, of course,
When a live Monk rides in upon a Mare,
Chase'd by a dead one, arm'd, upon a Horse.

Sir Thomas up to London sped, full fast,
To beg his life, and lands, of Royal Harry,
And, for his services, in Gallia, past,
His suit did not miscarry:—

For, in those days,—thank Heaven they are mended!—
Kings hang'd poor Rogues, while rich ones were befriended.
Ye Criticks, and ye Hyper-Criticks!—who
Have deign'd (in reading this my story thro')

A patient, or impatient, ear to lend me,—
If, as I humbly amble, ye complain
I give my Pegasus too loose a rein,
'Tis time to call my Betters to defend me.

Come, Swift! who made so merry with the Nine;
With thy far bolder Muse, Oh, shelter mine!
When she is style'd a slattern, and a trollop;—
Force stubborn Gravity to doff his gloom;
Point to thy Cælia, and thy Dressing-Room,
Thy Nymph at bed-time, and thy fame'd Maw-Wallop!

Come, Sterne!—whose prose, with all a Poet's art,
Tickles the fancy, while it melts the heart!—

Since at apologies I ne'er was handy,—
Come, while fastidious Readers run me hard,
And screen, sly playful wag! a hapless Bard,
Behind one volume of thy Tristram Shandy!

Ye Two, alone!—tho' I could bring a score
Of brilliant names, and high examples, more—
Plead for me, when 'tis said I misbehave me!
And, ye, sour Censors! in your crabbed fits,
Who will not let them rescue me as Wits,
Prithee, as Parsons, suffer 'em to save me!

THE ELDER BROTHER

Centrick, in London noise, and London follies,
Proud Covent Garden blooms, in smoky glory;
For chairmen, coffee-rooms, piazzas, dollies,
Cabbages, and comedians, fame'd in story!

 On this gay spot, (upon a sober plan,)
Dwelt a right regular, and staid, young man;—
Much did he early hours and quiet love;
And was entitle'd Mr. Isaac Shove.

An Orphan he;—yet rich in expectations,
(Which nobody seem'd likely to supplant,)
From, that prodigious bore of all relations,
A fusty, canting, stiff-rump'd Maiden Aunt:
The wealthy Miss Lucretia Cloghorty,—
Who had brought Isaac up, and own'd to forty.

Shove on this maiden's Will relied securely;
Who vow'd she ne'er would wed, to mar his riches;
Full often would she say of men demurely,—
"I can't abide the filthy things in breeches!"

 He had Apartments up two pair of stairs;
On the first floor lodge'd Doctor Crow;—
The Landlord was a torturer of hairs,
And made a grand display of wigs, below;
From the beau's Brutus, to the parson's grizzle:—
Over the door-way was his name;—'twas Twizzle.

Now, you must know,
This Doctor Crow
Was not of Law, nor Music, nor Divinity;—

He was obstetrick;—but, the fact is,
He didn't in Lucina's turnpike practise;
He took bye-roads,—reducing Ladies' shapes,
Who had secure'd themselves from leading apes,
But kept the reputation of virginity.

 Crow had a roomy tenement of brick,
Enclose'd with walls, one mile from Hyde Park corner;
Fir trees, and yews, were planted round it, thick;—
No situation was forlorner!
Yet, notwithstanding folks might scout it,
It suited qualmish Spinsters, who fell sick,
And didn't wish the world to know about it.

Here many a single gentlewoman came,
Pro tempore,—full tender of her fame!
Who, for a while, took leave of friends in town;—
"Business, forsooth! to Yorkshire call'd her down,
 Too weighty to be settle'd by Attorney!"—
And, in a month's, or six weeks' time, came back!
When every body cried, "Good lack!
How monstrous thin you've grown, upon your journey!"

The Doctor, knowing that a puff of Scandal
Would blow his private trade to tatters,
Dreaded to give the smallest handle
To those who dabble in their neighbours' matters;
Therefore, he wisely held it good
To hide his practice from the neighbourhood,
And not appear, there, as a resident;
But merely one who, casually, went
To see the lodgers in the large brick house;—
To lounge, and chat, not minding time a souse;—

 Like one to whom all business was quite foreign;—
And, thus, he visited his female sick;
Who lay as thick,
Within his tenement of brick,
As rabbits in a warren.

He lodge'd in Covent Garden all the while,
And, if they sent, in haste, for his assistance,
He soon was with 'em;—'twas no mighty distance;—
From the town's end it was but a bare mile.

Now Isaac Shove
Living above
This Doctor Crow,

And knowing Barber Twizzle live'd below,
Thought it might be as well,
Hearing so many knocks, single and double,

To buy, at his own cost, a street-door bell,
And save confusion, in the house, and trouble;

Whereby his (Isaac's) visitors might know,
Without long waiting in the dirt, and drizzle,
To ring for him at once;—and not to knock for Crow,—
Nor Twizzle.

Besides he now began to feel
The want of it was rather ungenteel;
For he had, often, thought it a disgrace
To hear, while sitting in his room, above,
Twizzle's shrill maid, on the first landing-place,
Screaming, "a man below vants Mister Shove!"
The bell was bought; the wire was made to steal
Round the dark stair-case, like a tortur'd eel,—

Twisting, and twining;
The jemmy handle Twizzle's door-post grace'd,
And, just beneath, a brazen plate was place'd,
Lacquer'd and shining;—

Graven whereon, in characters full clear,
And legible, did "Mr. Shove" appear;
And, furthermore, which you might read right well,
Was—"Please to ring the bell."

At half-past ten, precisely to a second,—
Shove, every night, his supper ended;
And sipp'd his glass of negus, till he reckon'd,
By his stop-watch, exactly, one more quarter;
Then, as exactly, he untied one garter;—
A token 'twas that he for bed intended:

Yet having, still, a quarter good before him,
He leisurely undress'd before the fire;
Contriving, as the quarter did expire,
To be as naked as his mother bore him:

Bating his shirt, and night-cap on his head;—
Then, as the watchman bawl'd eleven,
He had one foot in bed,
More certainly than cuckolds go to Heaven.

Alas! what pity 'tis that regularity,
Like Isaac Shove's, is such a rarity!

But there are swilling Wights, in London town,
Term'd—Jolly dogs,—Choice Spirits,—alias, Swine,
Who pour, in midnight revel, bumpers down,
Making their throats a thoroughfare for wine.

These spendthrifts, who Life's pleasures, thus, out-run,
Dozing, with head-aches, till the afternoon,
Lose half men's regular estate of Sun,
By borrowing, too largely, of the Moon.

One of this kidney,—Toby Tosspot hight,—
Was coming from the Bedford, late at night:

And being Bacchi plenus,—full of wine,—
Although he had a tolerable notion
Of aiming at progressive motion,
'Twasn't direct,—'twas serpentine,
He work'd, with sinuosities, along,
Like Monsieur Corkscrew worming thro' a Cork;
Not straight, like Corkscrew's proxy, stiff Don Prong,
A Fork.

At length, with near four bottles in his pate,
He saw the moon shining on Shove's brass plate;
When reading, "Please to ring the bell,"
And being civil, beyond measure,
"Ring it!"—says Toby—"very well;
I'll ring it with a deal of pleasure."

Toby, the kindest soul in all the town,
Gave it a jerk that almost jerk'd it down.
He waited full two minutes; no one came;
He waited full two minutes more; and then,—
Says Toby, "if he's deaf, I'm not to blame;
I'll pull it for the gentleman again."

But the first peal woke Isaac in a fright,
Who, quick as lightning, popping up his head,
Sat on his head's Antipodes, in bed,—
Pale as a parsnip,—bolt upright.

At length he, wisely, to himself did say,—
Calming his fears,—
"Tush!—'tis some fool has rung, and run away;"—
When peal the second rattle'd in his ears!

Shove jump'd into the middle of the floor;
And, trembling at each breath of air that stirr'd,
He grope'd down stairs, and open'd the street door,
While Toby was performing peal the third.

Isaac eye'd Toby, fearfully askant,—
And saw he was a strapper,—stout, and tall;
Then, put this question;—"Pray, Sir, what d'ye want?"
Says Toby,—"I want nothing, Sir, at all."

"Want nothing!—Sir, you've pull'd my bell, I vow,
As if you'd jerk it off the wire!"
Quoth Toby,—gravely making him a bow,—
"I pull'd it, Sir, at your desire."

"At mine!"—"Yes, yours—I hope I've done it well;
High time for bed, Sir; I was hast'ning to it;
But if you write up Please to ring the bell,
Common politeness makes me stop, and do it."

Isaac, now, waxing wroth apace,
Slamm'd the street door in Toby's face,
With all his might;
And Toby, as he shut it, swore
He was a dirty son of—something more
Than delicacy suffers me to write:

And, lifting up the knocker, gave a knock,
So long, and loud, it might have raise'd the dead;
Twizzle declares his house sustain'd a shock,
Enough to shake his lodgers out of bed.

Toby, his rage thus vented in the rap,
Went serpentining home, to take his nap.

'Tis, now, high time to let you know
That the obstetrick Doctor Crow
Awoke in the beginning of this matter,
By Toby's tintinnabulary clatter:

And, knowing that the bell belong'd to Shove,
He listen'd in his bed, but did not move;
He only did apostrophize;—
Sending to hell
Shove, and his bell,
That wouldn't let him close his eyes.

But when he heard a thundering knock,—says he,
"That's, certainly, a messenger for me;—
Somebody ill, in the Brick House, no doubt;"—
Then mutter'd, hurrying on his dressing-gown,
"I wish my Ladies, out of town,
Chose more convenient times for crying out!"

Crow, in the dark, now, reached the stair-case head;
Shove, in the dark, was coming up to bed.
 A combination of ideas flocking,
Upon the pericranium of Crow,—
Occasion'd by the hasty knocking,
Succeeded by a foot he heard below,—

He did, as many folks are apt to do,
Who argue in the dark, and in confusion;—
That is, from the Hypothesis, he drew
A false conclusion:

Concluding Shove to be the person sent,
With an express, from the brick tenement;
Whom Barber Twizzle, torturer of hairs,
Had, civilly, let in, and sent up stairs.

 As Shove came up, tho' he had, long time, kept
His character, for patience, very laudably,
He couldn't help, at every step he stepp'd,
Grunting, and grumbling, in his gizzard, audibly.

For Isaac's mental feelings, you must know,
Not only were considerably hurt,
But his corporeal, also—
Having no other clothing than a shirt;—
A dress, beyond all doubt, most light and airy,
It being, then, a frost in January.

When Shove was deep down stairs, the Doctor heard,
(Being much nearer the stair top,)
Just here and there, a random word,
Of the Soliloquies that Shove let drop;—

 But, shortly, by progression, brought
To contact nearer,
The Doctor, consequently, heard him clearer,—
And then the fag-end of this sentence caught:

Which Shove repeated warmly, tho' he shiver'd:—
"Damn Twizzle's house! and damn the Bell!

And damn the fool who rang it!—Well,
From all such plagues I'll quickly be deliver'd."

"What?—quickly be deliver'd!" echoes Crow;—
"Who is it?—Come, be sharp;—reply, reply;
Who wants to be deliver'd? let me know."
Recovering his surprise, Shove answer'd, "I."

"You be deliver'd!" says the Doctor,—"'Sblood!"
Hearing a man's gruff voice—"You lout! you lob!
You be deliver'd!—Come, that's very good!"
Says Shove, "I will, so help me Bob!"

"Fellow," cried Crow, "you're drunk with filthy beer!
A drunkard, fellow, is a brute's next neighbour;—
But Miss Cloghorty's time was very near,
And, I suppose, Lucretia's now in labour."

"Zounds!" bellows Shove, with rage and wonder wild,
"Why then, my maiden Aunt is big with child!"

Here was, at once, a sad discovery made!
Lucretia's frolick, now, was past a joke;—
Shove tremble'd for his Fortune, Crow, his Trade,
Both, both saw ruin,—by one fatal stroke;

But, with his Aunt, when Isaac did discuss,
She hush'd the matter up, by speaking thus:—

"Sweet Isaac!" said Lucretia, "spare my Fame!—
Tho', for my babe, I feel as should a mother,
Your Fortune will continue much the same;
For,—keep the Secret,—you're his Elder Brother."

George Colman the Younger – A Concise Bibliography

The Female Dramatist (1782)
Two to One (1784)
Turk and No Turk (1785)
Inkle and Yarico (1787)
Ways and Means (1788)
The Battle of Hexham (1793)
The Iron Chest (1796)
The Heir at Law (1797)
The Poor Gentleman (1802)
John Bull, or an Englishman's Fireside (1803)

Colman was also the author of a great deal of so-called humorous poetry (usually coarse, though popular) – My Night Gown and Slippers (1797), reprinted under the name of Broad Grins, in 1802; and Poetical Vagaries (1812). Some of his writings were published under the assumed name of Arthur Griffinhood of Turnham Green.